One Boy's JOURNEY

Rob Waring, *Series Editor*

NATIONAL GEOGRAPHIC
LEARNING

Australia · Brazil · Mexico · Singapore · United Kingdom · United States

Words to Know

This story is set in the African countries of Mali and Mauritania, near the Sahara Desert. It happens in the town of Diafarabe [dɪɑfərɑbeɪ] and across the Sahel [səheɪl] region.

(A) **Cattle Herding.** Read the paragraph. Then match each word or phrase with the correct definition.

The Fulani [fulɑni] are a group of people in Africa who raise cattle. Every year, young Fulani herdsmen take their cattle to an arid region near the Sahara Desert. There, they must find places for their cows to graze and get food. They must ensure that their dairy cows remain healthy and produce a lot of milk. It's a difficult job because cattle like a temperate climate, not hot and dry places.

1. cattle _____	**a.** a cow used for producing milk
2. herdsmen _____	**b.** very dry
3. arid _____	**c.** large farm animals kept for their milk or meat
4. graze _____	**d.** not very hot and not very cold
5. dairy cow _____	**e.** eat small amounts of food at a time
6. temperate climate _____	**f.** men or boys who care for groups of animals of the same type

The Arid Sahel Region

B **A Dangerous Journey.** Read about the dangers that the Fulani herdsmen meet. Then, write each underlined word or phrase next to the correct definition.

> Hyenas come out at night and try to kill the cattle.
> There are many mosquitoes which cause dangerous diseases.
> Cattle rustlers often try to take away the cattle.
> In some places, rebels are trying to take over the area.

1. people who steal cattle: _____

2. an insect which bites people and animals: _____

3. a wild animal from Africa and Asia that looks like a dog: _____

4. groups who are fighting against the people in power in a country: _____

A Mosquito

A Hyena

a herd of cattle

a Fulani herdsman

3

Yoro Sisse[1] is a 16-year-old Fulani boy from the town of Diafarabe. For thousands of years, Fulani boys, like Yoro, have made a very dangerous journey. They leave their girlfriends and their families behind in Diafarabe, and walk across the edge of the Sahara Desert. Why do they make this dangerous journey across this arid region? The main reason is simple: to feed their cattle.

---

[1] **Yoro Sisse:** [yɔrou sɪseɪ]

🎧 CD 2, Track 05

Skim for Gist

Read through the entire book quickly to answer the questions.

1. Why is Yoro's success very important?

2. Is Yoro successful on his journey?

At the end of the **dry season**,[2] Yoro and the other boys must take their cattle out of the **Inner Niger Delta**[3] and into the Sahel. Soon it will be too wet for the cattle in the delta. The herdsmen must travel with their cattle to find better grazing areas.

The Sahel is an arid region with very few plants and trees. It goes along the edge of the Sahara Desert, which spreads all the way across Africa. Cattle don't usually live well in arid places. They are animals that like a temperate climate, not dry desert. The success of the Fulani people is a direct result of their ability to raise cattle in an arid environment.

[2]**dry season:** a period of the year in which there is regularly very little rain
[3]**Inner Niger Delta:** [naɪdʒər dɛltə] a low, level land area near the Niger River in Mali

These young cattle herders live away from home with their cattle for up to eight months a year. While they are away, they live mainly on milk that is taken from their dairy cows.

Yoro explains what it's like to make this long and dangerous journey. According to him, the most important thing is to always **be focused on**[4] one thing—grazing. "We constantly have to find new grazing," he says. "That's what's always in your mind. In **the bush**[5] we have to be completely focused. Our **mission**[6] is to bring back fat cattle," he says. Bringing back fat cattle is very important for Yoro. Why? Because it may determine his future.

---

[4]**be focused on (something):** have one's attention on one particular thing
[5]**the bush:** an area of land which has never been farmed and where there are few people
[6]**mission:** main job; goal

For Yoro and other Fulani boys, bringing home a healthy herd is a traditional **rite of passage**.[7] If a Fulani boy returns with healthy cattle, then he is considered to be a man. When Yoro returns home to Diafarabe, the other Fulani people will look carefully at the cattle. They will check his work as a herdsman for the past eight months. They will then decide if he's capable of managing a herd properly.

Yoro's girlfriend, **Aissa**,[8] also hopes that he's done well. She has a good reason for doing so: she's now old enough to get married. In Fulani society, parents choose who their daughters and sons will marry. If Yoro doesn't bring his herd home in excellent condition, Aissa's parents probably won't choose him to be her husband.

---

[7] **rite of passage:** an activity which indicates an important stage in a person's life, especially when becoming an adult
[8] **Aissa:** [ɑisə]

During the journey, Yoro has to make sure that his cattle get enough food in the dry, desert environment. But that's not his only worry. There are also several other dangers. There are rebels and cattle rustlers. There are also dangerous mosquitoes that can cause serious diseases.

Yoro starts his journey in Diafarabe, Mali, and walks into Mauritania. He follows **routes**[9] that may have existed for thousands of years. They've been here since a time when people and cattle were first forced into the Sahel. As the Sahara region dried out and became a desert, the people that lived there had to leave. They had to find a more temperate climate in which to live.

---

[9]**route:** a particular way or direction between places

Yoro walks and walks. Then, after three months in the bush, it's finally time for him to turn and go home. It's been a difficult time for the young boy. "We walk from sunrise to sunset without stopping," he says. "Sometimes we get very thirsty and the cows get tired." He then adds, "Often we don't sleep at night." Why? That's when the hyenas come out. They might try to kill the young cows, or 'calves.' Yoro and the other herders often watch their cattle all night. They can't risk losing an animal now!

The last part of Yoro's journey is very difficult. It becomes almost like a forced march for him and the animals. Fortunately, Yoro's herd is doing well. There are many healthy calves and they need to be **branded**.[10] Putting his brand on the calves is a proud moment for Yoro. The calves immediately make his family richer and show Yoro's **courage**[11] and skill during the last eight months.

---

[10] **brand:** mark an animal, such as a cow, by burning its skin
[11] **courage:** the ability to control fear in a dangerous or difficult situation

Putting a brand on a calf is a proud moment for Fulani herdsmen.

Yoro is almost home now. He's so close he can almost see it, and he's really excited to see his girlfriend, Aissa. There's just one more challenge to his long journey. He must cross a dangerous river with his cattle. Yoro's cattle are his future and he wants to be sure of their safety. Because of this, he chooses to cross the river with them.

The cattle mean everything to Yoro. He chooses to cross the river with them to ensure their safety.

After the long journey, Yoro has brought home a healthy herd. Both he and Aissa can be proud of his success. It's time for a happy **celebration** [12] in Diafarabe.

Later, Yoro spends some time with Aissa. He tells her of his intention to marry her. Aissa is pleased, but it's Aissa's parents, not Aissa and Yoro, who will decide if they can marry. Yoro has done everything he can. His future, and Aissa's, are linked to the river and the land of the Sahel. They're also linked to the dangerous journey that young Fulani boys have made for thousands of years.

---

[12]**celebration:** a special social event, such as a party, to show that something is important

Summarize

Summarize the story of Yoro's journey. Tell it to a partner or write it in a notebook. Include the following information:

- Where did the journey take place?

- Why did he make the journey?

- What were some of the dangers he met?

- How will the journey affect him?

After You Read

1. On page 4, 'they' refers to Fulani:
   A. families
   B. boys
   C. girlfriends
   D. cows

2. Cattle usually prefer a _____ climate to a _____ one.
   A. warm, hot
   B. cold, wet
   C. dry, cool
   D. hot, wet

3. Match the cause to the effect.
   Effect: Fulani boys take cattle out of the Inner Niger Delta.
   A. People need food in the Sahel.
   B. The desert has no plants or trees.
   C. The dry season is ending.
   D. Fulani people are good with cattle.

4. The main purpose of Yoro's journey is to:
   A. marry his girlfriend
   B. survive the dangerous desert
   C. make a new mission
   D. return with healthy cattle

5. Which word on page 11 means 'cause'?
   A. reason
   B. check
   C. choose
   D. capable

6. Which of the following is NOT a good heading for page 11?
   A. Fulani Rites of Passage
   B. Will Yoro Become a Man?
   C. Aissa and Yoro Won't Marry
   D. Villagers Wait for Yoro

7. Which of the following is NOT a danger that Yoro faces?
    A. disease
    B. wind
    C. rustlers
    D. fighters

8. Yoro's way to Mauritania is:
    A. terrible
    B. modern
    C. short
    D. ancient

9. In paragraph 2 on page 14, the word 'forced' shows that Yoro and the cattle have NO:
    A. choice
    B. route
    C. goal
    D. benefit

10. The writer probably thinks Yoro is:
    A. weak
    B. serious
    C. strong
    D. childish

11. Which is a good heading for page 16?
    A. Yoro and Cattle Cross Road
    B. Long Journey Finally Begins
    C. Healthy Herd Changes Yoro's Past
    D. A Young Man Returns Home

12. What's the purpose of page 18?
    A. to show that Yoro won't marry Aissa
    B. to explain the effects of Yoro's journey on his future
    C. to teach the importance of listening to parents
    D. to show that Yoro is a special Fulani

The
BOOK BAG

by Joe and Tina Reed

The Real Cowboy Story

Cowboys have existed in the American west for almost 200 years. Thousands of books have been written about them. Who were the real cowboys and where are they today? Two writers share their views on this interesting subject in their new books. We've read them both and here's what we think.

RATING SCALE
Excellent ★★★★ Terrible ★

Thousands of books have been written about cowboys.

THE FIRST COWBOYS
by Carlos Carrillo, Cowboy Books, $39.95

The first half of Carlos Carrillo's new book seems like a novel. The year is 1600 and three young Spanish men have just arrived in 'New Spain' (what is now Mexico). They have come to be 'vaqueros.' (The exact meaning of this word in English is 'cow men,' which later became 'cowboy.') Carrillo follows Jose, Hector, and Pedro as they learn their skills. They move large herds of cows from place to place, control wild horses, and teach new cowboys everything they know. The second half of the book then describes the historical influence of the *vaqueros* in Mexican and American cultures. It also features some beautiful paintings and pencil drawings. The art and historical descriptions of the second half of the book really support the story in the beginning. Carillo does a great job of bringing the two together.

Interest Level ★★★★   *Art* ★★★
Historical Truth ★★   *Price* ★★

WHERE DID ALL THE COWBOYS GO?
by Rita Turnbell, Gorman Publishing, $12.95

In this carefully researched book, Rita Turnbell explains why there are so few cowboys left today. Before the late 1800s, the western part of the United States was mostly public land. As new Americans moved there to start farms, all the public land disappeared. Soon cowboys were no longer needed. The book explains in detail why the cowboys lost the ability to do their traditional work. It is full of facts and is a very good value for the money. However, the information could have been presented in a more interesting form. The writer should have given more personal information about the cowboys. She also could have included more artwork to support her points.
This book is an okay read.

CD 2, Track 06

Word Count: 340
Time: _____

Interest Level   ★   *Art*   ★
Historical Truth ★★★★   *Price* ★★★★

Vocabulary List

arid (2, 4, 7)
be focused on (something) (8)
brand (14, 15)
cattle (2, 3, 4, 7, 8, 11, 12, 14, 16, 17)
cattle rustler (3, 12)
celebration (18)
courage (14)
dairy cow (2, 8)
dry season (7)
graze (2, 7, 8)
herdsman (2, 3, 7, 11)
hyena (3, 14)
mission (8)
mosquito (3, 12)
rebel fighter (3, 12)
rite of passage (11)
route (12)
temperate climate (2, 7, 12)
the bush (8, 14)